FOLLOW THE LEADER STORIES

Courage, Esther!

CAROLYN NYSTROM

Illustrated by Sharon Dahl

MOODY PRESS

CHICAGO

Carolyn Nystrom is well known as the author of Moody Press's long-lived doctrinal series, Children's Bible Basics. She has written 64 books—some available in ten languages—as well as stories and curriculum material. A former elementary school teacher, she also served on the curriculum committee of her local school board.

Carolyn and her husband, Roger, live in St. Charles, Illinois, a Chicago suburb. As foster parents, they have cared for seven children in addition to their own two daughters. In her spare time, Carolyn enjoys hiking, classical music, gardening, aerobics, and making quilts.

Now award-winning artist Sharon Dahl has teamed up with Carolyn Nystrom to provide lively, captivating illustrations for the Follow the Leader Series. Sharon lives with her husband Gordon and daughters Samantha and Sydney in Boonton Township, New Jersey.

©1998 by
CAROLYN NYSTROM

Moody Press, a ministry of the Moody Bible Institute, is designed for education, evangelization, and edification. If we may assist you in knowing more about Christ and the Christian life, please write us without obligation: Moody Press, c/o MLM, Chicago, IL 60610.

ISBN: 0-8024-2206-3

1 3 5 7 9 10 8 6 4 2

Printed in the United States of America

I never wanted to be queen.
I was just a Jewish girl living with my cousin.
Each night he tucked me into bed and whispered in my ear,
"Jehovah is God."

But he never said those words out loud.
That would be dangerous.

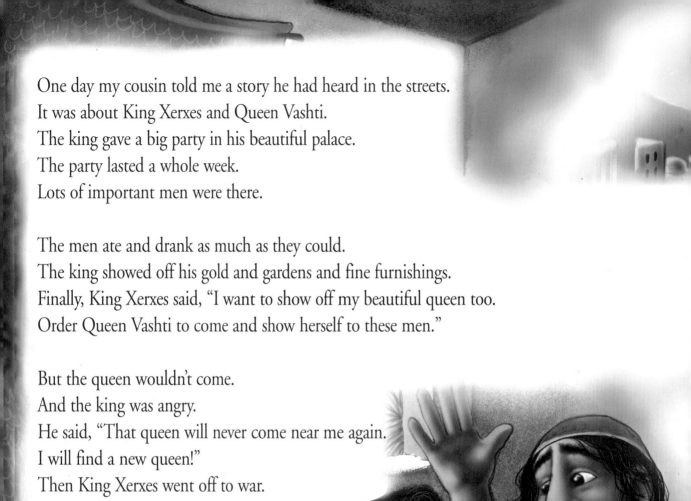

One day my cousin told me a story he had heard in the streets.
It was about King Xerxes and Queen Vashti.
The king gave a big party in his beautiful palace.
The party lasted a whole week.
Lots of important men were there.

The men ate and drank as much as they could.
The king showed off his gold and gardens and fine furnishings.
Finally, King Xerxes said, "I want to show off my beautiful queen too.
Order Queen Vashti to come and show herself to these men."

But the queen wouldn't come.
And the king was angry.
He said, "That queen will never come near me again.
I will find a new queen!"
Then King Xerxes went off to war.

When the king came back from war, I wasn't a little girl anymore.
I was a young woman, and people said I was beautiful.
The king had lost the war.
And he was still angry.
He sent men all over the country looking for a new queen.

The king's men caught me and hustled me off toward the palace.
They took lots of other girls too.
I was so scared that I could hardly walk,
but I held my head high.

"Courage, Esther," I heard a soft voice say.
My cousin Mordecai slipped out of the crowd.
"Jehovah is God," he whispered in my ear.
I nodded.
  "Don't tell that you are a Jew," he said. "That is dangerous.
    But don't forget that you belong to God."

For a whole year I lived with the other young women.
Servants gave us the best food.
Slaves covered us with lotions and paints and perfumes.
Maids brushed and combed our hair—
anything to make us more beautiful.
But we could not go to the king unless he ordered us.
No one could.

Some of the girls ran beauty contests.
They acted out what they would do when they met the king.
They pretended that they were queens already.

I thought that was all silly.
I didn't even want to be queen.
I didn't care if King Xerxes ever called for me.
But he did.

It wasn't easy to walk into the king's room.
Would he like me?
Would he send me away to live with his old women?
Would he get angry and have me killed?

"Courage, Esther," Cousin Mordecai had said.
I held my head high and walked in.

HE LIKED ME!
Ever so slightly, I tilted my head.
I felt him place a crown on my hair.

Then the king gave a big party
and told everyone that I was his new queen.
He even gave the whole country a holiday.

"I am Queen Esther to King Xerxes," I said.
I am also a Jew, and I belong to God, I whispered to myself.
But I didn't say those words out loud.
That would be dangerous.

Cousin Mordecai sat outside the palace gate.
He was not invited to the king's party.
But no matter where I went,
I knew that my cousin watched.
He wanted to be sure that I was safe.

One day, while sitting quietly at the gate,
Cousin Mordecai heard some scary news.
Two men planned to kill King Xerxes!

My cousin let me know.
And I told the king.
I also told him that a man named Mordecai had brought the message.

The king did not die—but the two men did.
And King Xerxes wrote my cousin's name in his book.

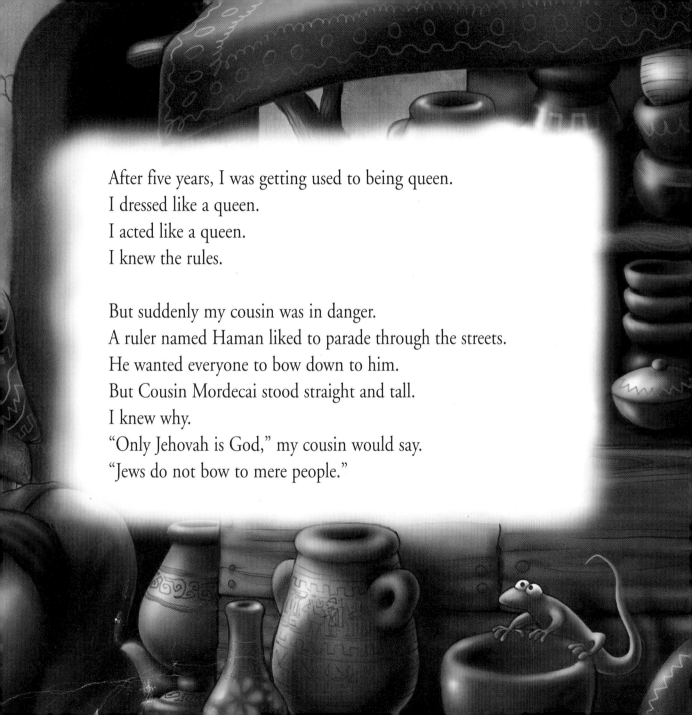

After five years, I was getting used to being queen.
I dressed like a queen.
I acted like a queen.
I knew the rules.

But suddenly my cousin was in danger.
A ruler named Haman liked to parade through the streets.
He wanted everyone to bow down to him.
But Cousin Mordecai stood straight and tall.
I knew why.
"Only Jehovah is God," my cousin would say.
"Jews do not bow to mere people."

Haman went to King Xerxes and complained.
"There is a group of people called Jews spread all over our country.
They are different from us.
They don't give proper respect to me.
Maybe they will not obey even the king.
We should kill them all."

"Do as you please," said King Xerxes.
And he sealed the order with his ring.
In eleven months all Jews would be dead.

My cousin sat at the gate and cried.

Then Cousin Mordecai sent me a message.
"Now is the time," he said.
"You must tell the king that you are Jewish."

I shivered.
"You know the rules," I answered.
"The king can kill anyone who comes to him without being called.
And he has not called me for a whole month!"

"Without your help, all Jews could die—even you," my cousin said.
"Maybe you are queen for just this reason."

"I'm so scared," I whispered.
"Pray for me. I will pray, too.
Ask all the people to stop eating and pray for three days."
My cousin nodded.

"Then I will go to the king," I said.
"If I die, I die."

"Courage, Esther," said my cousin.

Three days later I dressed in my most beautiful clothes.
I put my queen's crown on my head.
Then I stood in the inner court.
Would this be the last day that I lived?
Far away, I could see Xerxes on his throne.
What would he do when he saw me?

I wanted to run away, but I did not run.
I stood and waited.

I saw Xerxes move his eyes toward me.
I saw him shift his weight on his throne.
I held my breath.
Then I saw the king lift his golden scepter and hold it out.
I walked toward the throne and touched the end of his scepter.

"What do you want, my queen?" he asked.
"I would give you half of my kingdom."
Should I say it now? I thought.
No, now is not the time.

"Let's have a party," I said.
"Be sure to invite Haman."

I made a wonderful party.
We ate the best foods on gold plates.
We drank the best drinks from gold cups.
Haman sat right next to the king.

Once again the king asked, "What do you want, my queen?"
"I will give you half of my kingdom."

But I thought, *Now is not the time.*
Not yet.

So I said, "Please, my king, let's have another party.
Then I will answer your question.
Oh," I added, "don't forget to invite Haman."

All day Haman bragged,
"I went to a party at the palace.
I sat right next to the king.
Tonight I will go again."

Then Haman saw my cousin sitting at the gate.
"Surely that man will bow to me now," Haman said.
"I am important even to the king."
But Cousin Mordecai did not bow.

And Haman was furious.
"I won't wait eleven months to kill that man," Haman yelled.
"I will hang him tomorrow—right before the party."
And he built a high gallows to kill my cousin.

But the king could not sleep that night.
So he read the records of his kingdom.
"Who is this man Mordecai?" he asked.
"Who is this man who saved my life?
Did anyone give him a reward?"

"Let Haman come in," the king said next morning.

"I need your advice," the king told Haman.
"What should I do to reward a man that I really like?"

Who, me? Haman thought.
The king wants to give me a reward.
Inside, he smiled.

"Here is what you should do," Haman said.
"Give him your best robe and your best horse.
Have your best servant lead him through the streets.
Let your servant yell to everyone how wonderful this man is."

Ha, ha, Haman said to himself.
I get to ride a fancy horse.

"Find Mordecai," the king said.
"Do all that for him."

I made another party—just like the first.
Haman sat next to the king again.
But he did not seem happy.

Once again, the king asked,
"Queen Esther, you must tell me your wish.
I will give you half of my kingdom."

Now is the time, I thought.
Courage, Esther.

"Please, my king," I said.
"Please let me live.
And please spare the lives of my people."

"Whatever can you mean?" he asked.
"I am a Jew," I answered. "And so are my people."

I watched the king's face turn hard with anger.
"Who started all this trouble?" he shouted.

I stood tall and pointed.
"It is that wicked man Haman."

Everything changed quickly after that.
Haman was dead—on his own gallows.
The king chose my cousin as his most important help
My people were saved.
And Jews everywhere celebrated with a party.
They called it Purim.